1987

Dale and Janet,
 With love and Appreciation
Pastor and Mrs Brayman

good morning, LORD

Inspirations from Isaiah
Nelle A. Vander Ark

BAKER BOOK HOUSE
Grand Rapids, Michigan 49506

To
my sister Gertrude
and
my friend Dorothy
for all their love to me

Copyright 1980 by
Baker Book House Company
ISBN: 0-8010-9281-7

Printed in the United States of America

Unless otherwise indicated, all Scripture is taken from the New International Version, © 1978 New York International Bible Society, by the Zondervan Corporation, Grand Rapids, Michigan.

1
Meet Isaiah

The vision concerning Judah and Jerusalem that Isaiah son of Amoz saw during the reigns of Uzziah, Jotham, Ahaz and Hezekiah, kings of Judah.

Isa. 1:1

About 750 years before Christ, Isaiah, the prince of the prophets, appeared to God's people and preached the gospel in all its force and fulness. The message that Isaiah brought is the "old, old story" of sin and salvation—of God's just judgments and His wondrous mercy.

We know little or nothing about Isaiah's early life, but we can know everything about the way of life God revealed to Isaiah and empowered him to speak and to record.

Isaiah is not an easy book. It is like a mine that requires much digging and much refining; but it is a tremendously rich mine—inexhaustible in its treasure and worthy of any and all effort to learn what God told Isaiah. For the vision that God called Isaiah to speak to His people over two thousand years ago is the same message we need today, so that we may know God and His way of life—real life, unending life.

So, then, begin reading Isaiah as an adventure in living. Pray for enlightenment as you read, reflect upon the meaning for your life, resolve to put your enlightened faith to work, and pray as you go on your way that the light and truth that came to and through Isaiah may also be seen in you.

2
Picture Isaiah's Time

The vision concerning Judah and Jerusalem that Isaiah . . . saw during the reigns of Uzziah, Jotham, Ahaz and Hezekiah, kings of Judah.

Isa. 1:1

Isaiah's audience was the wayward nation of Israel. Long before Isaiah's time, God had said to Abraham: "I will make you into a great nation and I will bless you . . . and you will be a blessing" (Gen. 12:2). Abraham's descendants became the nation of Israel. But this nation, rather than influencing other nations and pointing them to the true God, was itself influenced by surrounding nations and even began to worship their gods. The people of Israel did not carry out God's directions. They refused to be a separated people, consecrated to the worship and the service of the one true God. They broke God's covenant with their father Abraham.

Isaiah was summoned to tell them forthrightly how their alliances with other nations were leading them to disaster. He was to warn them that their patronizing worship of Jehovah God would bring upon them His wrath and judgment.

Isaiah's message for God's people today is the same as it was in the days of the kings of Judah. It comes ringing through with passionate appeal: "Be what you were called to be! *Be a blessing!*" And to those who refuse or even neglect such a life, the warning of Isaiah still resounds loud and clear: "Woe to you!"

Isaiah's times are our times. Isaiah's message is the message of the ages: "Be a blessing or be accursed. Seek God's grace, or expect His judgment."

Dear God, the God of Abraham,
thank You that You always keep Your word.
Let Your grace flow to and through me
so that I need not fear Your wrath
but may enjoy the constant tenderness of Your
   love.
May I be a blessing today, Lord,
and thus show to others
how faithful, genuine, and kind You are.

3
Read Isaiah

Hear, O heavens! Listen, O earth!
For the Lord has spoken.

Isa. 1:2a

The best way to know a person is to listen to him. The best way to put a jigsaw puzzle together is first to see the picture on the box. The best way to travel through unfamiliar territory is to use a map. The way to understand a book is first to survey it and then to read it as a whole.

Isaiah was a real person who lived in an age similar to ours in many ways. We need to listen to him so that we may have the Lord's direction for our lives today. But in order to hear him most meaningfully and to understand the Lord's directions clearly, we need first to see the Book of Isaiah as a whole—to see "the picture on the box." And then to keep us on the track in our adventure through the book—to know where we are and where we are going—we need a map.

In selections 5, 7, and 9, I have outlined the main divisions of the book.* I encourage you to mark off in some way these divisions in your Bible, perhaps adding the headings in the margin so that these meditations can help you to "feed on" His word, rather than just nibble at it.

And as you walk along through Isaiah, sing and pray:

> Open my eyes that I may see
> Glimpses of truth Thou hast for me.
> Place in my hand the wonderful key
> That shall unclasp and set me free.
> Silently now I wait for Thee,
> Ready, my God, Thy will to see;
> Open my eyes—illumine me,
> Spirit divine!

---

*After von Orelli, quoted in H. C. Leupold, *Exposition of Isaiah* (Grand Rapids: Baker Book House, 1968), I.19.

4
Listen to Isaiah

He wakens me morning by morning,
wakens my ear to listen like one being taught.
                                                    Isa. 50:46

Do you have your Bible and your pencil or pen ready, for a survey and a sampling of the Book of Isaiah? The first twelve chapters constitute the first unit and may be divided into three sections. As I list the divisions in the next meditation, mark them in your Bible. Then *read* the selected Scripture passages for each division and sing the accompanying song. If you find it difficult to do all three divisions in one sitting, take only one. But read the Scripture passage and take time to think it through. It takes time to *feed* on God's word and to digest it so that it is absorbed into your life. "Take time to be holy," and take time to take time.

Pray that God will speak to you as you read and meditate. The Word of the Lord is still "the sword of the Spirit." It penetrates. It conquers!

Expect to see evidences of growth and fruitfulness as you discipline yourself in personal, regular Bible study. For God has promised through Isaiah:

> ... my word that goes out from my mouth:
> It will not return to me empty,
> but will accomplish what I desire
> and achieve the purpose for which I sent it.
> *Isa. 55:11*

So, then, to really learn from God through Isaiah, take the attitude of one who is being taught (see text at top of page). The first steps in your study are to read, write, and sing the main ideas in the book. And as you do this, follow the basic oft-repeated instruction of the divine teacher: "Pay attention! Listen to Me!"

"Listen to me, you who pursue righteousness and who seek the Lord" (Isa. 51:1a).

> Open my ears that I may hear
> Voices of truth Thou sendest clear.

5
Overview of Isaiah

PART 1

Chapters 1-12

1. **Prophecies concerning Judah and Jerusalem**
   A. Introduction and a typical message of Isaiah (chapter 1)
   Scripture: Isa. 1:10-20
   Song: "Though Your Sins Be as Scarlet"

   > Though your sins be as scarlet,
   > They shall be as white as snow.
   > Though your sins be as scarlet,
   > They shall be as white as snow.
   > Though they be red like crimson,
   > They shall be as wool.
   > Though your sins be as scarlet,
   > Though your sins be as scarlet,
   > They shall be as white as snow,
   > They shall be as white as snow.
   >
   > Hear the voice that entreats you,
   > O return ye unto God!
   > Hear the voice that entreats you,
   > O return ye unto God!
   > He is of great compassion,
   > And of wondrous love.
   > Hear the voice that entreats you,
   > Hear the voice that entreats you,
   > O return ye unto God!
   > O return ye unto God!

---

*Note: This overview in Scripture and in song, combined with the material on pp. 113-21, can be used very effectively as a unit for a worship service, or for an introductory lesson in a group Bible study of Isaiah.

B. Through judgment to the fulfillment of God's gracious promises (chapters 2–6)
Scripture: Isa. 5:1-7; 15-16
Song: "If We Have Forgotten the Name of our God" (metrical version of Ps. 44)

> If we have forgotten the Name of our God,
> Or unto an idol our hands spread abroad,
> Shall not the Almighty uncover this sin?
> He knows all our hearts and the secrets within.
>
> Refrain:
> Rise, help, and redeem us,
> Thy mercy we trust;
> Rise, help, and redeem us,
> Thy mercy we trust.

C. The Immanuel book (chapters 7–12)
Scripture: Isa. 9:1-7
Song: "Hark, the Herald Angels Sing" (Charles Wesley, 1739)

> Christ, by highest heaven adored,
> Christ, the Everlasting Lord!
> Late in time behold Him come,
> Offspring of the Virgin's womb.
> Veiled in flesh the Godhead see;
> Hail th' Incarnate Deity,
> Pleased as man with men to dwell,
> Jesus, our Emmanuel.
>
> Refrain:
> Hark! the herald angels sing,
> "Glory to the newborn King."

6
Sing with Isaiah!

The whole earth is at rest and quiet: they break forth into singing.

Isa. 14:7, trans. Leupold

On that day there will be a delightful vineyard—sing of it!

Isa. 27:2, trans. Leupold

And the ransomed of the Lord . . . will enter Zion with singing.

Isa. 35:10a

When I was a child, a seventeen-year-old girl in my home church died of typhoid fever. She had been rather wayward until her illness, but as she lay wrestling with this deadly disease, the Spirit of God wrestled with her soul. One morning near the end of her life she heard a familiar hymn on the radio: "We're Marching to Zion." As she listened, she was moved by the words in the second stanza:

> Let those refuse to sing
> Who never knew our God,
> But children of the heavenly King
> Must speak their joys abroad. . . .

She began to pray, "I've been refusing to sing the songs of heaven, but, O God, I was wrong. Now I want to sing Your songs more than anything else—today and always." The Lord spoke peace and pardon to her, and she sang the songs of heaven before the Lord took her from this life. At her funeral a large group of young people sang at her request all the stanzas of "We're Marching to Zion." The impression on me was indelible.

As I read and reread Isaiah, I know ever more fully why all God's creation sings (Isa. 24.7), why God's children can and must sing of His wondrous works (Ps. 96), and why "the ransomed of the Lord... will enter Zion with singing" (Isa. 35:10). The earth sings because it is restored to harmony with its Creator. God's people sing on earth because they recognize themselves as God's "delightful vineyard" (Isa. 27:2) once again made wonderfully fruitful, and they find in God all security and stability, protection, and purpose (Isa. 24–26). And beyond all that there is the prospect of triumph and everlasting life with God and the grand company of the redeemed (Isa. 35).

Yes, there is judgment in Isaiah, but the songs of salvation overpower the notes of condemnation. For the gospel according to Isaiah is the gospel of grace: "Where sin abounds, grace does much more abound."

Sing of this grace. Show God's salvation from day to day.

7
Overview of Isaiah
PART 2

Chapters 13-39

2. Oracles of judgment (chapters 13-27)
Scripture: Isa. 24:21-23; 25:1-9
Song: "A Shelter in the Time of Storm"

> The Lord's our Rock, in Him we hide,
> A shelter in the time of storm;
> Secure whatever ill betide,
> A shelter in the time of storm.
>
> A shade by day, defense by night,
> A shelter in the time of storm;
> No fears alarm, no foes affright,
> A shelter in the time of storm.
>
> Refrain:
> Oh, Jesus is a Rock in a weary land,
> A weary land, a weary land;
> Oh, Jesus is a Rock in a weary land,
> A shelter in the time of storm.

3. The Book of Zion (chapters 28-35)
Scripture: Isa. 35:1-10
Song: "We're Marching to Zion"

Come, we that love the Lord,
And let our joys be known,
Join in a song with sweet accord, (repeat)
And thus surround the throne. (repeat)

Refrain:
We're marching to Zion
Beautiful, beautiful Zion!
We're marching upward to Zion,
The beautiful city of God.

4. Historical interlude (chapters 36-39)
Scripture: Isa. 37:14-20
Song: "The Ends of All the Earth Shall Hear"
(metrical version of Ps. 22)

The ends of all the earth shall hear
And turn unto the Lord in fear;
All kindreds of the earth shall own
And worship Him as God alone.

Refrain:
All earth to Him her homage brings,
The Lord of lords, the Kings of kings.

8
Be Comforted by Isaiah

You who bring good tidings to Zion,
  go up on a high mountain.
You who bring good tidings to Jerusalem,
  lift up your voice with a shout,
lift it up, do not be afraid;
  say to the towns of Judah
    "Here is your God!"

Isa. 40:9

Isaiah is the book of consolation to God's people. To make this truth real for yourself, read several chapters from chapter 40 on, and underline all the references used to allay fear, such as: "Do not be afraid"; "do not fear" (or, "fear not"); "I am God"; "I am your God"; "I am with you"; "I will help [deliver] you."

As you note these statements, their context, and the promise associated with each one, waves of comfort will flood your soul. Indeed, you will have "comfort to spare."

There are so many reasons for comfort set forth in these passages. Briefly, let us look at three suggested by the line in the text above: "Here is your God!" First, then, God is; second, God is here; and this God is your God.

God is *God*. Isaiah is called to remind God's people over and over: "I [Yahweh] am God, and there is no other." (Read chapters 44, 45, and 46 especially for oft-repeated emphasis of this truth.) The eternal God, the living God, the God of the Scriptures says: "I am God. I create, I purpose, I keep." "What I have said, that will I bring about; what I have planned, that will I do" (Isa. 46:11b).

This God is *here*. He speaks. (Underscore the many times Isaiah writes: "This is what the Lord says.") You have heard him, haven't you? "I... speak the truth; I declare what is right" (Isa. 45:19b). He loves. He stays close. "Do not be afraid, for I am with you" (Isa. 43:5a). The God who speaks, the God who loves, and the God who stays close cannot be a distant God. No, the message of Isaiah is: "God comes to His people. God is here."

And, now the prophet invites the heralds to shout the good news from the mountain tops: "Here is *your* God" (my emphasis). Whose God? Your God, if you accept His invitation to "come near me and listen..." (Isa. 48:16).

Hear the voice that spoke to Isaiah, *and see* the God of all comfort.

9
Overview of Isaiah
PART 3

Chapters 40–66

5. **The Lord's measures for the deliverance of His people (chapters 40–48)**
   Scripture: Isa. 40:1-5
   Song: "Comfort, Comfort Ye My People (Johannes Olearius, 1671; trans. C. Winkworth, 1863)

   > Comfort, comfort ye My people,
   > Speak ye peace, thus saith our God;
   > Comfort those who sit in darkness,
   > Mourning 'neath their sorrow's load.
   > Speak ye to Jerusalem
   > Of the peace that waits for them;
   > Tell her that her sins I cover,
   > And her warfare now is over.

6. **The Lord's agent for the achieving of this work (chapters 49–57)**
   Scripture: Isa. 52:7-10; 53:1-6
   Song: "Ah, Dearest Jesus" (Johann Heerman, 1620; trans. Robert Bridges, 1899)

Ah, dearest Jesus, how hast Thou offended,
That man to judge thee hath in hate pretended?
By foes derided, by Thine own rejected,
   O most afflicted!

For me, dear Jesus, was Thine incarnation,
Thy mortal sorrow, and Thy life's oblation;
Thy death of anguish and Thy bitter passion,
   For my salvation.

7. The consummation of the Lord's salvation (chapters 58–66)

Scripture: Isa. 65:17-19
Song: "Jerusalem the Golden" (Bernard of Cluny, 12th century; trans. John M. Neale, 1851)

O sweet and blessed country, the home of God's elect!
O sweet and blessed country that eager hearts expect!
Jesus, in mercy bring us to that dear land of rest,
Who art, with God the Father and Spirit, ever blest.

10
When God Refuses to Listen

. . . even if you offer many prayers,
I will not listen.

Isa. 1:15b

Strange language, isn't it? Haven't we been taught that God hears and answers prayer and that, at times, even before we call, God answers (cf. Isa. 65:24a)?

Then when does God refuse to listen? When prayers are only words, with no intent to put them to work. I can well imagine (on the basis of Israel's prayer book, the Psalms) that a prayer commonly offered in Isaiah's day was: "Bless Your people, Lord. Give justice to all. Restore the afflicted. Remember the poor" (see Ps. 82:3-4).

Seems to me I have heard that prayer. In fact, I think I have prayed like that myself. I know I have. Then where do I stand, Lord? Are my prayers an offense to you? Will You refuse to listen to me?

And God replies, "Yes, *unless* you pledge yourself to seek the answer to your own prayers. When you pray for Me to bless others, then you must commit yourself to be a blessing to them. When you pray for justice for all, then pursue justice. When you pray for the oppressed and the poor, then go out and do everything you possibly can to relieve them, to meet their needs [cf. Isa. 1:17]. Then, as soon as I hear, I will answer you" (cf. Isa. 30:19b).

O God, teach me to pray, to mean what I say, and to give myself away today. Thank You, Lord, for tearing out all my pretenses and putting in me your genuineness. Fill me steadily with Your power—"power to pray and power to do."

> O Thou Fount of blessing,
> Purify my Spirit,
> Trusting only in Thy merit...
> And in all, great and small
> May I seek to do most nearly
> What Thou lovest dearly.
> *(Tersteegen and Miller)*

11
Let the Grace Flow

Take your evil deeds out of my sight!
Stop doing wrong, learn to do right!
Seek justice, encourage the oppressed. . . .

"Come now, let us reason together," says the Lord.
"Though your sins are like scarlet, they shall be as white as snow. . . .
If you are willing and obedient, you will eat the best from the land. . . .
For the mouth of the Lord has spoken.

Isa. 1:16-20

Isaiah steps on the stage and addresses God's chosen people with scathing words of judgment from the Lord. "Ah, sinful nation... brood of evildoers... you persist in rebellion.... Stop bringing meaningless offerings! Your incense is detestable to me.... I cannot bear your evil assemblies... your appointed feasts my soul hates" (cf. Isa. 1:4-14). I hate your so-called worship. I despise it. I can't stand it.

Remember to whom Isaiah is speaking—God's chosen people! They knew better, but they prostituted their knowledge. Their lives did not conform to what they knew. Thus God's judgment on them was severe.

We tend to say, "They had it coming. They knew

better. Such ingrates!" We recognize their emptiness in worship, their externalism, their inconsistencies, and we say, "Such hypocrites! No wonder God was angry!" But then we stop to think: Are there any modern parallels? Is our worship ever empty, a routine that has lost its force? Is going to church merely a part of our lifestyle? Or does something happen to us when we worship? Are we different the next day? Do we carry out God's concerns for justice and righteousness in the nitty-gritty of life? Are we willing to get our hands dirty to show how much God loves?

Who can stand in judgment over the Israelites? We see all too clearly our own guilt and our plight. What is the way out? Note Isaiah does not say, "The way out is to get your theology straight and to change your order of worship." No, he calls for repentance: Change your life!

How? The God who speaks to Israel (and to us) in anger for ignoring Him now comes in a "reasoning" love, pardon, and renewal. The first lesson in the new life is that we be "willing and obedient" (Isa. 1:19) to the grace of God. When the grace of God flows into us with its cleansing power, it will steadily flow through us so that everyone we meet may know God lives in us.

Let the grace flow, and thank God that He comes to us and lives in us.

12
Bitter Fruit

My loved one had a vineyard
  on a fertile hillside.
He dug it up and cleared it of stones
  and planted it with the choicest vines....
Then he looked for a crop of good grapes,
  but it yielded only bad fruit.

Isa. 5:1b-2

Imagine a vineyard keeper who selected a fertile spot for planting a new vineyard. He carefully prepared the soil, destroyed every weed, picked up all the stones or objects that would hinder growth, and then planted well-established, healthy vines. As the plants grew, the keeper tended them faithfully, watering and nourishing them regularly. He had every reason to expect that he would have a crop of the juiciest, sweetest grapes. As the first grapes began to ripen, he picked one and tasted it. To his dismay, he found that the fruit was bitter. He just could not eat it. The crop was totally unmarketable.

What went wrong? The keeper began to search for causes. As he looked around, he saw some wild vines in a neighboring field. He picked a bit of fruit from them. Ah, the same bitter taste that he found in his own grapes. Then he knew what happened. The strong pollen from the wild plants had blown upon his new vines and spoiled his crop.

The vineyard here is a picture of Israel (Isa. 5:7), God's people of all ages. God is the careful keeper, and He has every reason to expect a good crop. There are other "pollens" in the air, however. There are strong influences which may take over in the lives of God's people. The analogy breaks down here, however. In the parable, God's people are pictured as vines, but that picture cannot portray the whole of man. In reality, people are not mindless, powerless plants. God has made man a deciding creature, and by His grace has given man power to choose—to choose life, to reject evil influences, and to be an influence for good. He will thus produce sweet, ever-bearing fruit (Deut. 30:19-20).

Have you tasted any of the fruit of your life lately? What would God find if He took a taste of something that you produced?

13
"Root Rot" Is Deadly

*... their roots will decay
   and their flowers blow away like dust;
for they have rejected the law of the Lord Almighty
   and spurned the word of the Holy One of Israel.*

Isa. 5:24b

We have seen from the parable of the vineyard that the nation of Israel, though faithfully tended by God, produced bad fruit. Later in chapter 5 Isaiah lists their specific sins. A dismal picture develops as one "woe" follows the other.

Woe to the land-grabbers (v. 8).
Woe to those who run after their drinks or befog their senses so that they are blind to the purposes of God (v. 11-12).
Woe to those who entangle themselves in self-deception, taunting God to hurry and let them see His plan develop (v. 18-19).
Woe to those who have lost their sense of right and wrong—with no moral values left, only confusion and perversion (v. 20).
Woe to those who think they can run their own lives—those who "are wise in their own eyes" (v. 21).
Woe to those who boast of how much wine they

can take and how well they can mix drinks (v. 22).

Woe to the corrupt judges—"who acquit the guilty for a bribe, but deny justice to the innocent" (v. 23).

What a mess! Greed, aimlessness, deceit, no sense of morality or values, self-worship, drunkenness, bribery, and injustice—sin in every form and in every place.

But all of these sins resulted from one disease—decay at the root. The plant of Israel withered because the people refused to take in the nourishment prescribed and provided by the God who brought them into being and planted them in their land. "They have rejected the law of the Lord" (v. 24).

Check again the list of woes, and note how each sin is rooted in self. See how each evil stems from a self-indulging, self-directed attitude toward life rather than a spirit yielded to God and drawing upon Him for fruitfulness.

Israel's history is a solemn reminder to us that the destiny of mankind is always a matter of life or death. There is no middle ground. And the conditions for our destiny are rejection or acceptance of God's way. Reject God, feed on the world, and die. Accept God, feed on the Word, and live!

14
"I Saw the Lord"

In the year that King Uzziah died, I saw the Lord seated on a throne, high and exalted, and the train of his robe filled the temple. Above him were seraphs, each with six wings. . . .
And they were calling to one another:
  "Holy, holy, holy is the Lord Almighty;
    the whole earth is full of his glory."
At the sound of their voices the doorposts and thresholds shook and the temple was filled with smoke.

Isa. 6:1-4

Before Isaiah was commissioned, he was given a lesson in awe. Man is not very good at *awe*, it seems. The people at Sinai had to learn awe when God gave them the law. Job had to stop arguing with God and simply listen to God—in awe (cf. Job 38). The shepherds came to worship the Christ-child and are singled out for the unusual gift they brought—awe.

Isaiah needed to recapture the sense of awe of God before he could be God's messenger to God's people. For that purpose the Lord sent him a vision that transported him to another world.

What did he see? "I saw the Lord seated on a throne, high and exalted, and the train of his robe filled the temple" (Isa. 6:1b). "I saw the Lord . . .

high and exalted." And the Lord wore a robe whose splendor fell in cascades, and His glory streamed into the room so that there was no place for man to stand there. The angels around the Lord covered their faces with fear and their feet with humility, but kept one set of wings ready to speed away at the Lord's command. These seraphs sang to one another the praise of a thrice-holy God, whose glory filled the earth. When their voices sounded, the doors shook and smoke filled the building. What an awesome scene—the resplendent Lord, the thrilling song, frightening tremors, and billowing smoke!

What was God telling Isaiah? The answer can be found in the words: "I saw the Lord." Isaiah had to have a clear vision of God—the only God—before he could speak to God's people. He had to know this God as the Almighty One, the Exalted One, the perfectly holy One, who could tolerate no questions about His position nor any imperfections in His people. Isaiah had to see that this holy God pervades the creation; and that when He comes to earth and touches it, something happens. The world trembles at God's touch.

But God enabled Isaiah to rise and preach to that trembling world in the spirit of awe.

15
Burning Grace

"Woe to me!" I cried. "I am ruined! For I am a man of unclean lips, and I live among a people of unclean lips...."

Then one of the seraphs flew to me with a live coal in his hand.... With it he touched my mouth and said, "See, this has touched your lips; your guilt is taken away and your sin atoned for."

Then I heard the voice of the Lord saying, "Whom shall I send? And who will go for us?"

And I said, "Here am I. Send me!"

Isa. 6:5-8

When Isaiah "saw the Lord" (v. 1), he stood in awe, and he suddenly knew how little and how frail he was. With that knowledge came also a sense of falling apart—"Woe to me!... I am ruined!" (v. 5a). He became aware of his uncleanness, both personal and communal. "I am a man of unclean lips, and I live among a people of unclean lips" (v. 5b). He was overwhelmed by the awful distance between the perfect purity of God and the gross impurity of his own heart. In his helplessness and hopelessness, he cried out, "I am lost! How can such a holy God ever have anything to do with me—a thoroughly corrupt person? Surely judgment—woe—will fall upon me!"

Is there, then, no hope? Yes, there is, when God acts. Note the action in verses 6 and 7 above. One of the seraphs took a live coal from the altar, seared the prophet's lips with it, and pronounced him clean and free. But his lips had been burned! What a drastic action! Is there no easier way to change a man from uncleanness to cleanness?

No, there is no cheap grace; there is only a burning grace. God changes His people and makes them fit instruments for His use by burning grace. Burning grace changes us completely so that we who have come to see nothing in self can find everything in God.

Note how Isaiah changed after he once saw his lostness in the light of the holy God and then experienced pardon by the power of His burning grace. That grace prompted and qualified him to answer God's call for a messenger to His people: "Here am I. Send me!"

If we have caught the vision of who God is and who we are before Him and have been burned by His renewing and equipping grace, we, too, are qualified to go and tell the story of God's transforming love.

> Touch my silent lips, O Lord
> And my mouth shall praise accord...
> Sinners, then, shall learn from me
> And return, O God, to Thee.
>
> *(metrical version of Ps. 51)*

16
His Name Is Wonderful

. . . and He will be called Wonderful. . . .
Isa. 9:6b

When we speak of something so delightful that we almost run out of words to describe it, we say, "It's wonderful!" Even more so do we, who by God's grace have come to know and love Jesus Christ, say of Him, "He's wonderful!"

What's so wonderful about Him? Who is He and what has He done to arouse within us such a sense of excitement, admiration, and awe?

To answer those questions we need to reflect a bit upon our sense of wonder. What is it, and how is it aroused? Wonder is a God-given capacity to be excited by something new, to gaze admiringly at something beautiful, and to be awed by something mysterious.

We see much of this faculty in children, for they still dare to express their spontaneous delight in something new, beautiful, or amazing. Surely part of their childlikeness that Christ recommends for all of us is to keep our sense of wonder alive and to let it show.

The prophet Isaiah nourishes our sense of wonder and directs it toward a proper object when he says of Jesus Christ, "and He will be called Wonderful." In the next pages, we will explore the above characteristics of wonder as applied to the Savior: newness, beauty, and mystery.

To prepare for this adventure, trace the use of the words *wonder*, *wonderful*, and *wondering* in the Scripture. (For example, see Isa. 25:11, Ps. 139:6, Luke 2:18, Matt. 7:28, and Mark 11:28.) Pray as you read that the Lord will revive your sense of wonder, for wonder is the first stage in learning. When we begin to wonder, we begin to inquire. And inquiry leads us to know more of why Christ is called Wonderful—and to delight in that Name.

17
The Wonder of the New
PART 1

... and He will be called Wonderful....
Isa. 9:6b

... I am making everything new!
Rev. 21:5a

Jesus Christ is wonderful because He is new. He is new in the sense that He brought to earth a new thought of God. To some the concept Jesus brought was not completely new. But it had almost faded. He came to renew and demonstrate what the prophets and the psalmists had spoken of as the substance for a "new song."

Before Christ came, the prevailing belief was in gods created in man's image, after his imagination—not according to God's revelation. These gods were thought of as ferocious beings to be appeased. The supreme quality of these gods was their superhuman strength: they were tyrants.

Then Jesus Christ came and gave to mankind a

new (or renewed) concept—God as Father. It was Jesus who revealed and openly demonstrated the possibility of a close, tender, personal relationship with a loving, heavenly Father. That was new to many and almost lost to those who once knew it. Jesus brought the Father to light (John 1).

Those of us who have been raised in the church may need to reflect on the newness of Christ's ideas—how revolutionary was His teaching. We tend to forget that until Jesus came, very few people thought of God as a Father or One interested in persons as individuals. Before Christ's coming, men thought of God as a judge—and indeed He is. But Jesus came as the Word to communicate to man the fulness of God's nature, both as a judge and as a deliverer. He showed us a God who, as a Father, grieves over His lost children and delights in every single one who comes to Him. That revelation of God was new. And Jesus is wonderful!

18
The Wonder of the New
PART 2

... and He will be called Wonderful....

Isa. 9:6b

When a Samaritan woman came to draw water, Jesus said to her, "Will you give me a drink?"

John 4:7

Jesus is wonderful not only because He brought to light a new revelation of God, but also because from Him we gain a new conception of man. Oh, yes, the belief that man was made "a little less than God" (Ps. 8:5, RSV) was proclaimed centuries before Christ, but as years passed, man lost the proper view of man. Human life became cheap. Many of the sports in the ancient world were nothing more than murderous combats between men and animals. In fact, frequently the animals were considered to be more valuable than people.

Jesus came, and life acquired a new sacredness. Heathenism deified strength and looked upon the physically weak, such as women and children, with contempt. Jesus introduced a new order. He embraced children and recognized women as being as much "happy objects of His grace" as men. He restored to the world the value of human life.

Christ made it very clear in His ministry that God loves man. Say those wonderful words again: "For God so loved the world that he gave his one and only Son, that whoever believes in him shall not perish but have eternal life" (John 3:16). Thus, man has value, not because of what he is, but because God loves him.

Oh, the wonder of the newness that Christ brought to earth! He taught anew that God is a Father, that man is a person whom God loves, and that those who come to Christ can enjoy life with God again—now and always!

> O the wonder of it all, the wonder of it all,
> Just to think that God loves me.
>
> *G. B. Shea*

19
The Wonder of the Beautiful

... and He will be called Wonderful Counselor ... Everlasting Father. ...

Isa. 9:6b

We have seen his glory, the glory of the one and only Son, who came from the Father, full of grace and truth.

John 1:14b

Wonder is excited by the new. It is also aroused in the presence of the beautiful and the magnificent. Wonder then takes on the quality of admiration.

The person named by Isaiah came to earth as a man, Jesus Christ. Note well: Jesus is a man, a human being. While He was on earth, He showed Himself to be a wonderful man—a beautiful person. He knew exactly how to befriend the friendless and how to help each person in distress, even though such unqualified compassion brought bitter criticism. He also knew when to speak out and when to keep silent. He was wonderful in His concern and magnificent in His wisdom.

He showed Himself to be the "altogether lovely One." His character had no weak points, no deficiencies, no excesses. He proved in His ministry on earth (and He continues to show us) that He is a "marvel of a counselor" and "everlastingly a father." As such, He perfectly demonstrated both discernment (justice) and mercy. While both mercy and justice, love and truth, are manifest in Christ, never does one prevail at the expense of the other. Christ is never so merciful as to deny justice, or so just as to make mercy impossible. Where can you find that beautiful balance except in Jesus? He is magnificent. He is wonderful!

The person and the character of Jesus is not only beautifully balanced but also complete. In Him is every element of moral and spiritual beauty. Read the record of His life honestly, and ponder the testimony of those who observed Him every day: "We have seen his glory... full of grace and truth."

Yes, look anew at Christ. Then stand back in wonder, in admiration, and in worship. And as you look and look at Jesus Christ, you will be moved to say, "My God, how wonderful Thou art!"

20
The Wonder of the Mysterious
PART 1

And he will be called Wonderful Counselor, Mighty God. . . .

Isa. 9:6b

Jesus is wonderful, and part of the reason He arouses our wonder is that He is mysterious. There is mystery in the completeness and the magnificence of His life. There is further mystery in His person. Jesus is man, but He is also God. Two natures—the human and the divine—bound together to constitute one person. Yet Jesus acts, not with a double mind or a conflicting spirit, but with a single consciousness and a single will. How can that be? We cannot understand it. If we could explain it, we would be as great as He. We can accept it, however, as a great mystery and see it by faith as the marvelous way God provided to pay for our sins and to deliver us from the prisons we built for ourselves.

Yes, the revelation of the two natures of Christ is one of the greatest mysteries in the whole plan of salvation. We stand in awe at the wonder of it all, and we sing:

> His name is Wonderful,
> His name is Wonderful,
> His name is Wonderful,
> Jesus, my Lord.
> He is the mighty King,
> Master of everything;
> His name is Wonderful,
> Jesus, my Lord.
> He's the great Shepherd,
> The Rock of all ages,
> Almighty God is He.
> Bow down before Him;
> Love and adore Him,
> His name is Wonderful,
> Jesus, my Lord.*

---

*"His Name Is Wonderful," by Audrey Mieir, Copyright 1959 by Marina Music, Inc., Burbank, California.

21
The Wonder of the Mysterious
PART 2

And he will be called Wonderful... Prince of Peace.

Isa. 9:6b

Amazing love, how can it be
That Thou, my God, should'st die for me!

Ponder that thought. It's awesome. How wonderful that my God died for me!

Recently I learned of someone who had spent several months in the hospital. Her condition required extensive, delicate surgery and months of intensive care. This was followed by weeks of costly therapy and rehabilitation. The total bill for the medical services, the hospital care, and the subsequent therapy was nearly seventy thousand dollars. As I reflected on that, one thought came to me repeatedly: "What a cost to save a life! What a tremendous investment in one person!"

But as I continued thinking, I was struck by this

fact: God has much more than seventy thousand dollars invested in me. What God has done for me goes far beyond any mathematical figure. God gave His life for me. My God died so that I could live! O what wonder! How amazing!

Why did the Lord Jesus die? To pay the price of God's judgment for man's sin—the death sentence—and thus restore peace between God and man. Peace—the togetherness of that which belongs together. God and man belong together. When man broke the relationship, God sent Christ to heal the brokenness and to put man back together with God. He brought peace on earth again.

Think of all that Christ did. He paid the highest price, His own life, to bring about the highest good—peace with God. No wonder He is called the *Prince* of Peace. We bow in the blessed mystery of it all.

"Peace to all of you who are in Christ" I Peter 5:14b.

22
Come Singing and Go Singing

"Surely God is my salvation;
I will trust and not be afraid.
The Lord, the Lord, is my strength and my song;
he has become my salvation."
With joy you will draw water
from the wells of salvation.

Isa. 12:2-3

This passage is one of my favorite texts, and is probably enjoyed by many other believers, too. It contains all the substance for life and all the elements of song.

Picture the wells in the country where Isaiah lived. Some of them are still being used today. The women of the villages and the surrounding countryside go to the wells several times a day to draw water and fill their jars. This is a happy task for them. People who have visited this ancient land report that those who come to draw water from the wells *come singing and leave singing*.

How fitting, then, is this picture in describing what happens as we travel the dusty, wearisome ways of life. We feel the need for deliverance and renewal (that is, salvation)—freedom from guilt, from fear, from weakness, from depression of spirit. How can we find such relief? By being led by God—away from all that which is wearing and back to that which is renewing and as refreshing as a cold drink on a hot day. We need an "exodus" such as the Lord provides for all who will follow Him. Then we can sing again the refrain of the first "exodus" (Exod. 15:2) and the chant of the exiles returning from captivity (Ps. 118:14):

> The Lord is my strength and my song;
> he has become my salvation.

So, sing with eagerness as you come to God. Fill every container you possess with water from God's well, drink and drink of the "living water" Christ gives (John 4:10-14), and go on your way again singing, revived and satisfied.

> Out of my bondage, sorrow and night,
> Jesus, I come; Jesus, I come;
> Into thy freedom, gladness and light,
> Jesus, I come to Thee.
>
> *Wm. T. Sleeper*

23
Get Excited about Your Faith!

*Shout aloud and sing for joy, people of Zion,
for great is the Holy One of Israel among you.*
                                                        Isa. 12:6

At a recent worship service the minister brought a stimulating message on the promise of God to Abram from Gen. 15:5: "Look at the heavens and count the stars—if indeed you can count them.... So shall your offspring be." We in the congregation were challenged to believe God, even when we cannot see or understand—we are to take God at His word. Then the minister clearly set forth the work of the church: "Go out with the same faith and vision of Abraham. Go out and count the stars, and let your faith be as big as the promises of God. Believe God that as countless as the stars will be the multitudes who come to believe in Jesus Christ, the great descendant of Abraham. Remember that this Jesus arose from the dead and is the ultimate, living proof that God keeps His word. Believe God and tell the world about Him and the risen Christ."

Then came the time for the congregation to respond. The words of the Apostles' Creed were spoken in unison. Beautiful words, throbbing with life. "I believe... I believe... I believe..." But what I heard was not a joyous shout—it was a seemingly perfunctory, half-voiced sound. There was no excitement, no life, no apparent conviction in it. At that point I could almost hear Isaiah say, "Shout aloud, you people, for you have a great God!"

Oh, how much we need to get more excited about our faith today! We can have dreams of great missionary endeavors, carefully structured programs, and give much money for spreading the good news of salvation throughout the world, but the impetus for it all must start with people who are so excited about their faith that they cannot keep it to themselves.

Isaiah said this over and over (42:10–11; 44:23; 45:8; 48:20–21; 49:13; 52:7–10). May God give us the desire and the courage to confess our faith loud and clear and joyously "shout, for the blessed Jesus reigns."

24
To God Be the Glory

Lord, you establish peace for us;
all that we have accomplished you have done for us.
O Lord, our God, other lords besides you have ruled over us,
but your name alone do we honor.

Isa. 26:12-13

A brilliant young pianist appeared in his final college concert. He paused to address a few words to the audience before he began to play. He spoke of his love for the piano and what playing it had done for him throughout the years but how he lost his zeal for it for a time. Then he testified of a quickening of his desire to be the best pianist he could possibly be and to play the best in music for the piano. The renewal of spirit, he said, began with a fresh, wholehearted desire to "do all to the glory of God." He said, "I don't really know what that means, but somehow I feel that I can really please God now by playing the piano, and I want to do just that tonight—play to the glory of God tonight—whatever that means."

And he sat down quietly and played his instrument so masterfully and sensitively that the audience was moved to worship along with him.

"'To the glory of God'—whatever that means." What does it mean? It's scriptural language, and we use the phrase frequently. What does it really mean?

The above text suggests two main elements in living "to the glory of God": recognition of who God is and what He has done, and wholehearted expression of our grateful tribute. It's a matter of seeing more and more of God's *attributes* and constantly *attributing* to Him all that is due Him for the wonders of His grace. The young pianist was right in saying, "I don't really know what it means to do all to the glory of God, but I'll just start by cultivating my God-given talents with full recognition of and endless thanks to the Giver."

Israel repeatedly had to learn who was the Source of her life and the Power of all her accomplishments, and to "give God the glory."

> All that I am I owe to Thee,
> Thy wisdom, Lord, has fashioned me;
> I give my Maker thankful praise,
> Whose wondrous works my soul amaze.
> *(metrical version of Ps. 139)*

25
God Is a Good Farmer

*Caraway is not threshed with a sledge,
    nor is a cartwheel rolled over cummin;
caraway is beaten out with a rod,
    and cummin with a stick.*

*... All this also comes from the Lord Almighty,
    wonderful in counsel and magnificent in wisdom.*

Isa. 28:27, 29

Lest God and His ways be misunderstood by His people, He lets the prophet provide a parable to make plain what He is doing. In this parable (v. 24ff.) God is pictured as a farmer as he prepares the soil wisely, sows sensibly, and harvests carefully.

Take a special look at the harvesting methods described in the above texts. You have all seen caraway seed—a small, delicate spice sometimes added to cheese or to rye bread. Cummin is also a small seed, similar to dill. "Now," God says, "you know that farmers don't harvest caraway seed by beating it out with a sledge hammer or thresh cummin by riding over it with a wagon wheel. No, they suit the threshing instrument to the material.

Surely, I, the Teacher of farmers (v. 26) will pay close attention to what kind of crop I am harvesting. I do not design to pulverize the seed but to release it and to use it in the best possible way."

Seems like such a simple lesson, doesn't it? But what a depth of comfort is packed into that illustration. The Lord will not deal too severely with His people, even though they have been recalcitrant and deserve no special consideration. He does not aim to wreck lives but to salvage them, for He is "wonderful in counsel and magnificent in wisdom" (v. 29b).

In Isaiah's day the faithful "remnant" who lived in the thick of a very complex situation needed such assurance. The same comfort still holds today. All who recognize their folly and insufficiency and come to God penitently and expectantly may be assured of His saving grace and His keeping power.

> The Lord upholds the faltering feet
> And makes the weak securely stand;
> The burdened ones, bowed down with grief,
> Are helped by His most gracious hand.
> *(metrical version of Ps. 145)*

26
Worship Without Heart

The Lord says:
 "These people come near to me with their mouth
 and honor me with their lips,
 but their hearts are far from me.
 Their worship of me is made up only of rules taught by men."

Isa. 29:13

One morning in church I observed an eleven- or twelve-year-old girl who was seated directly in front of me. She was toying with five "honor cards"—a type of award from Sunday school, I gathered. As the service progressed, the child's behavior distracted me. She paged through her Sunday school paper until her mother reached over and took it from her. The girl fretted for a few minutes, and then, in open defiance of her mother, pulled out part of another Sunday school paper and began working a crossword puzzle. All the while she made no attempt to participate in the worship—not in listening nor in singing. There was dishonor to parent and to God, but the honor cards were kept out in the open. You see why this was disturbing—honor cards in the hand but seemingly no real sense of honor in the heart.

My first reaction was to cast judgment on the child. Later I reflected on the incident in a broader light. How much of our lives too may be a substitution or a display of *form* (such as a card) for *reality*? Aren't we often like those addressed in the above text, or like those whom Paul described in his letter to Timothy as "having the *form* of godliness but denying the *power* thereof"? For example, we may pay our respects at a funeral home and even express sympathy and yet not remember the sorrowing ones the day after the funeral. Or, again, we would be very quick to say "Excuse me" or "I'm sorry" if we spilled on someone's clothes. Would we do the same if we soiled his name?

When and where is our godliness more show than substance, more lip than heart, more form than power?

27
Worship at Work

And [to] foreigners who bind themselves to the Lord to serve him, to love the name of the Lord, and to worship him, . . . these I will bring to my holy mountain and give them joy. . . .

Isa. 56:6a, 7a *(my emphasis)*

In everyday life, what is it to "love the name of the Lord," and what is it "to worship him" (v. 6a)? We say we must love God with all our heart, with all our soul, with all our mind, and with all our strength.

With all our heart and all our soul. With that confession on our lips, do we then live and work with integrity? Do we practice what we believe? Do we exemplify the truth that one's relationship to God is the only thing that really counts?

With all our mind. Do we have a clear understanding of our task, the people with whom we work, and our goals?

With all our strength. Do we live, work, and serve with interest, with a contagious enthusiasm?

And then, if we "love the name of the Lord," we say we must love our neighbor as ourselves. Do we demonstrate the reality of this confession by genuine graciousness, control of tongue and temper, and a compassionate concern for the discouraged and the troubled?

What a program! We check on ourselves and we cry: "Lord, who is equal to these things?" And the Lord replies, "I am."

"I am the Lord. . . . There is no God apart from me, a righteous God and a Savior. . . . Turn to me and be saved. . . . They will say of me, 'In the Lord alone are righteousness and strength'" (Isa. 45:18b, 21b, 22a, 24a).

"It is the Sovereign Lord who helps me. . ." (Isa. 50:9a).

So then, what is it to "love the name of the Lord and to worship him" as our text enjoins? We begin to see that, following an acknowledgment of the Lord God as the only God, there must be a commitment to work for Him in love and in His strength. And such work is part of our worship. Then, to those who work in love and faithfulness to God and thus worship as they work, the Lord promises an eternity of joyful worship at work—"these will I bring to my holy mountain and give them joy" (Isa. 56:7a).

28
The Road to Heaven

And a highway will be there;
 it will be called the Way of Holiness.
The unclean will not journey on it;
 it will be for those who walk in that Way;
 wicked fools will not go about on it.
 [Or—the simple will not stray from it.]
No lion will be there,
 nor will any ferocious beast get up on it....
But only the redeemed will walk there,
 and the ransomed of the Lord will return.
They will enter Zion....

Isa. 35:8-10a

In ancient days, roads in the Holy Land were mere trails. But the road described in this passage is more than a trail; it is a special highway—a road with a name and definite features, a passage that accommodates only certain travelers, and a way that leads to a single destination.

What is its name? The Way of Holiness, or the Holy Way. What a strange name! Roads are usually public and often named for a public figure. But this one suggests some privacy, separation from the usual traffic. *Holiness*—set aside for a special purpose. Sounds like strains from some of God's commands to His people: "Come out from among them, and be ye separate" (II Cor. 6:17a, KJV). "Ye shall be holy, for I the Lord your God am holy" (Lev. 19:2, KJV).

Besides its unusual name, what special features will this road have? It will be so clearly marked that no one traveling it will ever lose his way—not even the simple or the inexperienced (see the alternate reading of v. 8b, in brackets). Never to get lost on a desert road was almost incredible. Besides, this road will have none of the usual dangers of the wilderness—no lions or ferocious beasts on it (cf. v. 9).

Who is going to travel this road? "It will be for those who walk in that Way" (v. 8b); ". . . only the redeemed will walk there, and the ransomed of the Lord will return" (v. 9b). Only the redeemed, the ransomed. Who are they? Those who have acknowledged that "each of us has turned to his own way" (Isa. 53:6b), have found that way led to destruction. Then they returned to God's way, the only way that leads to *life* (cf. Isa. 35:7).

How can I find God's way? How can I join the redeemed and travel the road to heaven? Hear Christ speak: *Come to Me.* "I am the way" (John 14:6a). "Return to me, for I have redeemed you" (Isa. 44:22b). *Come, walk with Me.*

"All the way from earth to heaven I will guide you . . ."

29
Heaven

They will enter Zion with singing;
everlasting joy will crown their heads.
Gladness and joy will overtake them,
and sorrow and sighing will flee away.
Isa. 35:10b; 51:11b

As the captives were to return to Jerusalem, so the people of God of all ages will enter the place God has prepared for them—heaven. Heaven, like the return from captivity, is very real, and the sure prospect of going there inspires hope and joy.

Heaven is so far from our earthly thinking that the Bible uses figures to help us understand a bit of what is in store for us and to free our imagination to dream of our wondrous future.

What is heaven? Like Zion was for the captives, heaven is the end of our travels, the "city" which we call home and want to live in more than in any place this world could offer us. Heaven is the *embodiment* of all the blessings that God has prepared for His people. It is the place where God and His people live and work together in perfect love.

Those who are on the way to heaven, like the captives returning from exile, are aware of their coming blessedness. As they anticipate the fulfillment of all their hopes, they sing, jubilantly, triumphantly. With songs of victory, they enter the city.

And there "everlasting joy will crown their heads." The joy of the Lord, of which they sang for years on earth, is now so real that it encircles them like a crown on their heads. They feel regal and they revel in their royal state. They are kings and queens of the Most High God—not just for a day but always! "... *Everlasting* joy will be theirs" (Isa. 61:7c, my emphasis). Now since they have arrived at the city and been honored with crowns of joy, they need no longer pursue happiness. "Gladness and joy will overtake them."

"And sorrow and sighing will flee away." *Heaven is a way of life that means no more tears.* The prophet loves to remind us of that truth. Listen to Him: "The Sovereign Lord will wipe away the tears from all faces" (Isa. 25:8a).

> I will rejoice over Jerusalem
>   and take delight in my people;
>   the sound of weeping and of crying
>   will be heard in it no more.
>
> *Isa. 65:19*

> Jesus, in mercy bring us
> To that dear land of rest,
> Who art, with God the Father
> And Spirit, ever blest.
>   *(Bernard of Cluny, twelfth century)*

30
The Voice of Comfort

Comfort, comfort my people,
  says your God.
Speak tenderly to Jerusalem,
  and proclaim to her
that her hard service has been completed,
  that her sin has been paid for,
that she has received from the Lord's hand
  double for all her sins.

Isa. 40:1–2

Someone has said that it was the work of the prophets to "afflict the comfortable and to comfort the afflicted." With the above words the Book of Isaiah moves into the comfort section, filled with consolation and hope.

God speaks here not only to the prophet, it seems, but to any and all who spread the good news. Imagine someone coming to you in the midst of your grief, penitence, and anxiety, taking your hand, and saying to you over and over: "It's all right now. All will be well again. God is not holding your sin against you anymore. He sent me to tell you that He has forgiven you. God loves you. He is going to make you better than ever. Now relax. Rest in God's arms. He's taking care of everything."

But there is more to the message. Read the above

text again. Note well the words: *comfort, comfort* and *speak tenderly*.

Comfort. We usually think of this as something soft and soothing. And God does quiet His people; but He also quickens them. The second half of the word *comfort* suggests *fort, fortress, fortitude*. So then this text may well read: "Fortify, fortify my people, but do so tenderly."

Speak tenderly. We know that that is—"as a mother stills her child," as Christ Himself spoke to those who came for healing. "Speak tenderly"—as a soothing balm that is poured on an ache or a wound. Lay those blessed words of comfort on the heart and know that God Himself, the One whom you offended, is speaking comfort to you. And when God, the Covenant-God, brings comfort, it heals completely and it strengthens eternally.

> Comfort, comfort ye my people,
> Speak ye peace, thus saith our God;
> Comfort those who sit in darkness
> Mourning neath their sorrow's load.
> Speak ye to Jerusalem
> Of the peace that waits for them;
> Tell her that her sins I cover,
> And her warfare now is over.
>
> *(Johannes Olearius, 1671)*

31
The Voice of Preparation

A voice of one calling:
"In the desert prepare
  the way for the Lord,
make straight in the wilderness
  a highway for our God.
Every valley shall be raised up,
  every mountain and hill made low;
the rough ground shall become level,
  the rugged places a plain.
And the glory of the Lord will be revealed,
  and all mankind together will see it.
    For the mouth of the Lord has spoken."

Isa. 40:3-5

The King is coming. Prepare! Get the road ready for Him. You may expect Him to come by way of the wilderness. He honors you by coming; you honor Him by making a highway fit for a king. Fill in the valleys; level off the mountains; make steep ground level; make rough spots smooth.

The language of this passage is exuberant. The picture of a highway to be built is in keeping with what was done in Isaiah's days to welcome a new leader or conquering hero. It is a picture of what God's people need to do spiritually to prepare for the coming of their Deliverer. Every barrier, every obstacle to His coming, must be crushed to bits.

The way must be open for the Lord to come to His people. The real mountains are the apathy and the indifference of the people. The "leveler" is God's judgment, sent to jar His people out of their complacency.

How, then, shall full preparation be made for the coming King? John the Baptist, "the voice in the wilderness," answered that question. He preached the only way: "Repent" (Matt. 3:2). And then, "Produce fruit in keeping with repentance" (Luke 3:8a).

> For the herald's voice is crying
> In the desert far and near,
> Bidding all men to repentance,
> Since the kingdom now is here.
> O that warning cry obey!
> Now prepare for God a way;
> Let the valleys rise to meet Him
> And the hills bow down to greet Him.
>
> Make ye straight what long was crooked,
> Make the rougher places plain;
> Let your hearts be true and humble,
> As befits His holy reign.
> For the glory of the Lord
> Now o'er earth is shed abroad;
> And all flesh shall see the token
> That His Word is never broken.
>
> *(Johannes Olearius, 1671)*

32
The Voice of Warning

A voice says, "Cry out."
  And I said, "What shall I cry?"
"All men are like grass,
  and all their glory is like the flowers of the field.
The grass withers and the flowers fall,
  because the breath of the Lord blows on them.
  Surely the people are grass.
The grass withers and the flowers fall,
  but the word of our God stands forever."

Isa. 40:6–8

"Cry out."
"What shall I cry?"
"All men are like grass. . . .
The grass withers and the flowers fall. . . ."

What is the connection between this voice and the preceding one in Isaiah 40? God's great work of restoration has just been revealed. So now why the emphasis on the frailty of man? Israel needed to be warned not to begin again to build in, or on, its own strength. God repeatedly comes to His people to show them their weakness, their total inadequacy, and to warn them that it takes more than human resources to build anything lasting in the kingdom of God. The psalmists speak of man's frailty:

> You sweep men away in the sleep of death;
> they are like the new grass of the morning—
> though in the morning it springs up new,
> by evening it is dry and withered.
>
> *Ps. 90:5–6*

Peter echoes the words from Isaiah:

> All men are like grass...
> the grass withers and the flowers fall....
>
> *I Peter 1:24*

We cannot escape the force of the mournful cadence: The grass withers and the flowers fall....

But, thank God, the message does not end there. There is a firm foundation on which to build; there is a strength in which to live; there is a power that endures. "... The word of our God stands forever" (v. 8b).

So, then, rise and build, people of God. Build not in, or on, your own strength but on the prophetic Word of God. After all, that Word became flesh (John 1:14), and declared for all to hear in all times and places: "Heaven and earth will pass away, but my words will never pass away" (Matt. 24:35; Mark 13:31; Luke 21:33).

33
The Voice of Good News

You who bring good tidings to Zion,
  go up on a high mountain.
You who bring good tidings to Jerusalem,
  lift up your voice with a shout,
lift it up, do not be afraid;
  say to the towns of Judah,
    "Here is your God!"
See, the Sovereign Lord comes with power,
  and his arm rules for him.
See, his reward is with him,
  and his recompense accompanies him.
He tends his flock like a shepherd:
  He gathers the lambs in his arms
and carries them close to his heart;
  he gently leads those that have young.

Isa. 40:9-11

> Go, tell it on the mountain,
> Over the hills and everywhere;
> Go, tell it on the mountain
> That Jesus Christ is born.

This American folk hymn captures the spirit and the central message of the above passage in Isaiah. The herald was told to climb to the top of the mountain and to shout to the whole land of dispirited people, "God is here! God is here! God has come to help us! He is right here among us!"

But how would they recognize Him? What kind of person should they look for?

First of all, He will be a Conqueror—"conquering now and still to conquer." "See, the Sovereign Lord comes with power, and his arm rules for him" (v. 10a). His strength is invincible. His victory is sure. And you may be sure, fearful people, that His "reward" or "recompense" is with Him. This Conquering Hero will bring with Him His people, whom He has delivered from their enemies. See Him as the Mighty Conqueror!

But, see Him also as a tender Shepherd. He leads, never drives. He picks up the fearful, faltering lambs and "carries them close to his heart." He takes special care of those with special needs. He cares—He really cares. He is the Good Shepherd. He "lays down his life for the sheep" (John 10:11b).

Believe this good news, and then "go, tell it on the mountain!" Tell it for all the world to hear that God is here, that God triumphs, and God loves—tenderly and eternally!

34
The Incomparable God

To whom, then, will you compare God?
Isa. 40:18a

When the prophet came to Israel with almost unbelievable promises of restoration, the people must have wondered, "But who is going to accomplish all this? No nation has ever returned from a captivity and survived. How can we?"

To that question the prophet replied, "Consider the incomparable greatness of your God."

Look at your God over against the world He has created (Isa. 40:12-14).

> Who has measured the waters...
> or weighed the mountains? (v. 12)

Now look at your God over against the nations of the earth (vv. 15-17).

> Surely the nations are like a drop in the bucket...
> (v.15)

Then think of Him in contrast to the idols (vv. 18-20).

> What image will you compare him to? (v. 18b)

Here the prophet says in effect, "You make beautiful golden idols, decked with silver jewelry. Or, you try to find some wood that will not rot and erect a structure that will not topple" (cf. v. 20). Gold wears thin, silver tarnishes, wood rots, idols tumble but God....

Consider Him in contrast to the mighty of the earth (vv. 21–24).

> He brings princes to naught.... (v. 21)

Where are the Pharaohs? Where are the kings who once seemed so great to you?

If all that is not enough to strengthen your fainting spirit, then look at the stars.

> Lift your eyes and look to the heavens:
>   Who created all these?
> He who brings out the starry host one by one,
>   and calls them each by name.... (v. 26)

Who controls the affairs of men? Not the stars, as the Babylonians taught you. No, your God made the stars, and He directs them and calls each one by name night after night, and "not one of them is missing" (v. 26c). He has never lost one—not one of all the countless stars. Shall He not much more keep you, O you of little faith?

Consider the mountains, the nations, the idols, the kings, and the stars. "To whom, then, will you compare God?" (v. 18a).

35
Cries of the Troubled

Why do you say, O Jacob,
  and complain, O Israel,
"My way is hidden from the Lord;
  my cause is disregarded by my God"?

Isa. 40:27

Have you ever wondered what the people of Israel used as songs and prayers to express their distress during their days of captivity? Of course, one does not need a written prayer to express the anguish of the soul, but often in times of distress one recalls songs or prayers learned in childhood. Surely the captive Israelites must have reflected often on some of the psalms well known in their tradition. There is a line in the above text that sounds so much like one from the Psalms: "My way is hidden from the Lord."

The fear that God is hiding, that God is far away, that God does not really care any more is common in affliction. The psalmists spoke of that distress over and over. Listen to them cry:

Do not hide your face from me,
  do not turn your servant away in anger;
  you have been my helper.

Ps. 27:9

> Why do you hide your face
> and forget our misery and oppression?
>
> *Ps. 44:24*

> Do not hide your face from your servant;
> answer me quickly, for I am in trouble.
>
> *Ps. 69:17*

> Why, O Lord, do you reject me
> and hide your face from me?
>
> *Ps. 88:14*

Cries, cries of anguish! Over and over the psalmists and the captives cried: "O Lord, do not hide! O God, do not forsake us! How long, O Lord, must we wait? Why do you seem so far away? Have you forgotten us?"

Have you ever prayed like that? Aren't you glad those cries and questions are in the Bible? May God's people cry to their God and tell Him exactly how they feel? Of course. We may and we ought to complain *to* God, but we ought not to complain *about* God. But even when we do that, God comes to us, as He did in Israel's day, with His grace of correction (v. 27) and reassurance of His unfailing love. "Before they call, I will answer..." (Isa. 65:24a).

36
God's Answer to the Anxious

Do you not know?
  Have you not heard?
The Lord is the everlasting God,
  the Creator of the ends of the earth.
He will not grow tired or weary,
  and his understanding no one can fathom.
He gives strength to the weary
  and increases the power of the weak.

Isa. 40:28–29

O anxious ones, are you doubting the faithfulness and the strength of the Lord, your God? Remember who your God is.

"The Lord is the everlasting God" (v. 28a). "Have you not heard?" Moses spoke of your everlastingly loving God years ago: "The *eternal* God is your refuge, and underneath are the *everlasting* arms" (Deut. 33:27a). Do you not remember?

Your God is "the Creator of the ends of the earth" (v. 28a). "Have you not heard?" Moses told of it: "In the beginning God created the heavens and the earth" (Gen. 1:1). David sang of Him:

> He set the earth on its foundations;
>   it can never be moved.
>
> Ps. 104:5

Do you not remember? Do you not know that the Lord, your God, called the whole universe into being? Is it then conceivable that He Who made the world and everything that is in it should lack the power to control it? Or, do you perhaps think that this mighty Creator has forgotten to be kind? Do you not know:

> As a father has compassion on his children,
>   so the Lord has compassion on those who fear him;
> for he knows how we are formed,
>   he remembers that we are dust.
>
> Ps. 103:13–14

Do you not remember?

Are you troubled about your lack of strength? "Do you not know? Have you not heard?" Have you forgotten that the Almighty God of all creation not only has all strength but He also supplies it? Remember the song of the Exodus? "The Lord is my strength and my song" (Exod. 15:2a). That Lord is the everlasting God. He is God today, and He will strengthen you: "He gives strength to the weary..." (v. 29a).

O people of God, fearful and anxious, do you not know—your God?

37
Soar as an Eagle

*Even youths grow tired and weary,
  and young men stumble and fall;
but those who hope in the Lord
  will renew their strength.
They will soar on wings like eagles;
  they will run and not grow weary,
  they will walk and not be faint.*

Isa. 40:30-31

This is probably one of the most quoted texts in all of Scripture. It is important to note that it appears at the end of a great chapter on comfort. Divine comfort. As we noted in the meditation "The Voice of Comfort," pp. 62–63, *comfort* means more than quietude. It also means *fortitude*, strength for going on.

How is this strength gained? Note how human effort falters and fails. "Even youths grow tired and weary, and young men stumble and fall" (v. 30). More than the vigor of youth is needed to run the race of life. What is the secret of renewed courage (fortitude) and persevering strength? How shall we obtain it? Our God says, "Borrow it. Borrow it from Me."

"What? Borrow it, Lord? I want to be able to do things for myself. I want to run my own life. I want to be a model of strength."

And God says, "That's just exactly your problem. Remember you or anything you make is not your god and cannot be depended on. I am your God. I made you and made you to be dependent upon Me. Now, abandon self and come to Me; seek Me; look to Me; wait for Me; trust Me. Count on Me. Lean hard on Me. I will never fail you."

"Lord, I come. Renew me. Fortify me. Strengthen me."

"I will. Do not fear... for I am your God. I will strengthen you and help you; I will uphold you with my righteous right hand" (Isa. 41:10). "Now arise, go, for this is no place to rest. Use your wings and fly!"

Soar like the eagle and sing with the angels: "The Lord, the Lord, is my strength and my song" (Isa. 12:2b).

38
"Sing, Ye Islands of the Sea"

Sing to the Lord a new song,
  his praise from the ends of the earth,
you who go down to the sea, and all that is in it,
  you islands, and all who live in them.

Isa. 42:10

So often in Scripture a new work that God does is greeted with a new song. Check the Psalms for support of that statement. As you look up the following references, read each aloud, and then note the specific works of God which call for celebration with a new song. As your read each verse and note from the context the various reasons for joy, your spirit will sing anew and you will feel as if you have bathed in praise. See Psalms 33:3; 40:3; 96:1; 98:1; 144:9; and 149:1.

Oh, "how vast the benefits divine that we in Christ possess!" The blessings are not only numerous and varied but far-reaching—universal. In the text above and the following verses, you will note that praise will come "from the ends of the earth"—from the sea, from the islands, from the deserts, from the hidden cliffs, and from the mountaintops. Why? Because the Covenant-God is true to His word. He sent His Servant, as He said He would, and this Servant proved to be the Healer of all ills and the Deliverer from all oppression—the perfectly beautiful Savior and the Lord of the nations.

Jesus Christ, the Messiah, came. He invites all people everywhere to learn to know Him and enjoy the life that He has to offer. Then He commands all creation to "burst into songs of joy... for the Lord has comforted his people, he has redeemed Jerusalem... and all the ends of the earth will see the salvation of our God" (Isa. 52:9–10b).

> Sing, ye islands of the sea;
> Echo back, ye ocean caves;
> Earth shall keep her jubilee;
> Jesus saves! Jesus saves!

39
Think!

No one stops to think....
Isa. 44:19a

One of my favorite assignments after the first few lessons in a new semester's course is simply: "Now think! Just think." Many students first respond with a baffled look as if to say, "You're not serious, are you?" And then they leave the classroom with a kind of ease, almost an indifference, that seems to suggest, "Well, I guess we don't have any assignment for tomorrow."

"No assignment!" I then say to myself, "I've just given you the most demanding and most necessary task in all of learning and in all of life, and you failed to see it."

God must have felt something of that same dismay and, in addition, a lot of hurt and anger, when He saw His people making their own gods, gods out of pieces of metal or blocks of wood, and praying to these senseless things. Imagine asking a stick or a stone to bless you! What a stupid thing to do! And these were the people whom God had created, whom He had brought up, and through whom He promised to bless all other peoples. No wonder He sent His prophet to denounce them when He saw their folly in worshiping not the God who made them but the gods that they themselves had made.

But along with the accusation—"No one stops to think"—comes the gracious invitation to stop to think, to think anew with their Maker, to "reason together" again with their God, the only God (1:18); and to return to Him in whom alone is life (44:21-22).

The God of Israel still looks down with clear and searching eye on all that dwell below (see Ps. 33). I wonder how much non-thinking, thinking, and re-thinking He sees.

> O God, deliver me from my unthinking ways,
> from bowing down to something I have made
> or some idea I have dreamed up without You.
> Make me think, Lord, think with You,
> whatever the cost.
> And give me the grace
> to say "Amen" to this request.

40
Ask God to Carry You

Bel bows down, Nebo stoops,
  their idols are on beasts and cattle;
these things you carry are loaded
  as burdens on weary beasts.
They stoop, they bow down together,
  they cannot save the burden,
  but themselves go into captivity.

Hearken to me, O house of Jacob,
  all the remnant of the house of Israel,
who have been borne by me from your birth,
  carried from the womb;
even to your old age I am He,
  and to gray hairs I will carry you.
I have made, and I will bear;
  I will carry and will save.

Isa. 46:1-4, RSV

What a striking difference between false gods and the true God! Note again the picture in the above passage. Idols must be carried, and they fall down along with those who carry them. The true God does the carrying. He carries those who come to Him and holds them with a strong arm and unfaltering step from birth to death.

What a tremendous comfort is wrapped up in these words: "I will carry you!" (v. 4). God is not a detached spectator, who sees us struggle but remains uninvolved. No, He is like a loving mother to a child or a devoted husband to a wife (Isa. 54:6). He is keenly sensitive to our needs and willing and able to take care of us, completely and lastingly.

Is there then anything for us to do? Yes, we must come to God as a tired child coming to a loving parent and say, "Carry me." This simple act is the initial step in expressing and cultivating a child-like faith in God. The fundamental relationship to God is always one of surrender first—giving everything over to God and letting Him carry it all.

Ask God to carry you and all the heavy things you may be carrying around with you. Let Him lift all the things that weigh you down—the burdens of guilt, disillusionment, disappointment, sorrow, and grief. God is a caring and carrying God. We can trust Him to take over and to free us from all cares, for He sent Christ to be our burden-bearer. "Surely He has borne our griefs and carried our sorrows" (Isa. 53:4a).

> Ask the Savior to help you,
> Comfort, strengthen, and keep you.
> He is willing to aid you;
> He will carry you through.

41
If Only You Had...
But by Grace You Have

If only you had paid attention to my commands, your peace would have been like a river....
Isa. 48:18

If only! If only I had taken the time.... If only I had listened.... If only I had thought.... If only I had spoken.... Oh, how true it is:

> Of all the words of tongue or pen
> The saddest are these: it might have been!

O Israel, if only you had listened to Me! I told your father Abraham and I kept telling you through my prophets that you were My people, that I, and I alone, was your God, and that you had a special calling—to be a blessing, to be an influence for good and not to be influenced by any evil thing, by any foolish thought, or any foreign model. But you would not listen!

Jesus said, "O Jerusalem, Jerusalem, you who kill the prophets and stone those sent to you, how often I have longed to gather your children together, as a hen gathers her chicks under her wings, but you were not willing" (Matt. 23:37).

> How then can we be saved?
> Isa. 64:5c

"The Redeemer will come to Zion,
to those in Jacob who repent of their sins,"
   declares the Lord.

Isa. 59:20

"Rejoice with Jerusalem and be glad for her. . . .
I will extend peace to her like a river."

Isa. 66:10a, 12a

>Come to the Savior now
>Ye who have wandered far;
>Renew your solemn vow
>For His by right you are.
>Come like poor wandering sheep,
>Returning to His fold;
>His arm will safely keep,
>His love will ne'er grow cold.
>
>Come to the Savior now!
>He offers all to thee,
>And in His merits thou
>Hast an unfailing plea.
>No vain excuses frame,
>For feelings do not stay;
>None who to Jesus came
>Were ever sent away.
>
>*(John M. Wigner, 1844–1911)*

42
But What If God Forgets?

But Zion said, ". . . the Lord has forgotten me."
". . . I will not forget you!
See, I have engraved you on the palms of my hands."

Isa. 49:14-16

A joyous message has just been sent forth:

Shout for joy, O heavens;
    rejoice, O earth;
    burst into song, O mountains!
For the Lord comforts his people
    and will have compassion on his afflicted ones.

Isa. 49:13

But once again fear arises and doubt sets in. Instead of a song of joy there is a cry of anguish. ". . . Zion said, . . . 'The Lord has forgotten me'" (v. 14).

At this point one would expect the Lord to lose patience and to scold His people. But the Lord once again proves Himself to be abundantly gracious and long-suffering. He replies ever so reassuringly, "Can a mother forget the baby at her breast and have no compassion on the child she has borne? Though she may forget, I will not forget you!" (v. 15).

Yes, mothers have been known to forget their

own children, but God never forgets those who belong to Him. Note how emphatically He says: "I will not forget you!" (v. 15b). And then to underscore that promise, He uses a figure of speech. "See, I have engraved you on the palms of my hands" (v. 16). It is as though the Lord had deeply engraved or tattooed the name, or a picture, of Israel on the palms of His hands so that He could just sit and look at the names or the faces of His loved ones and continually be reminded of them. "Forget you, my dear people? No, I have made sure that I will always remember you." What could be more permanent than an engraving and more visible than the palms of the hand?

God still speaks to the troubled hearts of all His children today. "Don't worry. I will not forget you. I have your name and your face engraved in the palm of my hand."

Hard to believe that at times, isn't it? But isn't it a wonderful truth to dwell on? And when we do, we can smile and sing again.

> I am in my Father's keeping;
>   I am in His tender care.
> Whether waking, whether sleeping,
>   I am in His care.

43
Beautiful Feet

> How beautiful on the mountains
>   are the feet of those who bring good news,
> who proclaim peace,
>   who bring good tidings,
>   who proclaim salvation,
> who say to Zion,
>   "Your God reigns!"
>
> *Isa. 52:7*

Picture a crowd of people gathered in the land of Palestine, anxiously waiting for a report. The questions they ask are, "How is it going with the captives in Babylon? Has anybody heard anything? Do you think they will be freed?" Then suddenly just over the mountains to the east comes a runner. He must be the messenger with a report. He is running eagerly. He is speeding along. Look at those beautiful feet, running ever so lightly and ever so glad. He must have good news. As the messenger comes within shouting distance, his first cry is, "It's good. Good news! Good news!" He continues to call as he approaches; the announcements come tumbling out: "Good news! Peace! The captives are saved! They are delivered!" And as he nears the end of his joyous run and comes close to the crowd, he sums up his message in one grand declaration: "Your God proved Himself King. Your God reigns!"

Now the whole crowd breaks out into a loud shout of joy: "Hallelujah!" And shouts of joy rise from their hearts and lips: "Surely this is our God; we trusted in him, and he saved us. This is the Lord, we trusted in him; let us rejoice and be glad in his salvation" (Isa. 25:9). "God's favor is upon us once more. God has come back to His people. God is with us" (cf. Isa. 40:9). And they called upon all of the people and even the ruins to join them: "Burst into songs of joy together, you ruins of Jerusalem..." (Isa. 52:9a).

Why all this exuberance? "For the Lord has comforted his people; he has redeemed Jerusalem" (v. 9b), "... and all the ends of the earth will see the salvation of our God" (v. 10b).

Those beautiful feet still come running to us today telling us: "Good news! Your God came to save you, and your God reigns!"

"Shout, for the blessed Jesus reigns!"

44
He Is Not What We Expected

He was despised and rejected by men....
                                    Isa. 53:3a

How often we eagerly look forward to an event, and yet when it happens, we are keenly disappointed. That kind of built-up expectation and total disappointment accounts, in part, for the rejected and crucified Savior.

Trace briefly the building of expectations for a Messiah all through the Old Testament. In Genesis 3:15 mankind is given the great expectation that evil will some day be defeated. Steadily that expectation got more content. Abraham received the promise that through his descendants all the nations would be blessed. David sang of a great King to come and an eternal kingdom built on righteousness and justice. (Pss. 110, 72, 89, 96-99). Isaiah prophesied of a Wonderful Counsellor (Isa. 9:6) and of a coming utopia (Isa. 11). The people were built up to expect that the Messiah would be the fulfillment of all human needs and hopes.

But then why did they reject and despise the long-expected Messiah? Something had gone wrong with their expectations. They had become corrupted—corrupted with self-interest. When Jesus came, the Jews expected to *get ahead* through the Messiah, both nationally and personally. They expected Jesus to establish a kingdom that would blast Rome to bits and cause all the nations to recognize the Jewish nation as the leading world power. And the disciples expected to be leaders in that kingdom.

What did Jesus do? He did not build strong nationalism; instead He started associating with the despised Samaritans. He never talked about defeating the Romans, but rather about bringing light and healing to all peoples. When the disciples talked about being leaders in His kingdom and getting ahead personally, Jesus took out a towel and began to wash their feet. Imagine! They expected a sword and Jesus pulled out a towel! They expected a proud conqueror, and Jesus came as humble servant.

What disappointment! All expectations frustrated and hopes dashed! And because Jesus, the Messiah of God, was not what men wanted, "He was despised and rejected by men..." (v. 3a). From one point of view, Jesus Christ is crucified as the disclosure of what men do not want. The cross is an exhibition that says to all the world: "This Person is not wanted. Away with Him!"

Shall I crucify my Savior? Forbid, Lord. Cleanse me from self-interested expectations.

45
"That Your Soul May Live"

Hear me, that your soul may live.
Isa. 55:3a

Scene I
The time: About 600 B.C.
The place: Babylon
The characters: Hebrew captives
The situation: The people are working every day. They have plenty to eat and drink. They have some money and many things that money can buy.

Yet, there is something missing. The people are not happy. There is a gnawing hunger of the heart. There is an inner thirst. Life is dry. The spirit is withering. There is a sense of futility, a restlessness, an emptiness.

Life is a tread-mill existence.

Scene II
The time: Nearly A.D. 2000
The place: America
The characters: Citizens in a free land
The situation: The people work but have lots of time for play. They are preoccupied with making money. They spend hours every day eating, drinking, and spending. They have more money than ever before and are constantly acquiring more things that money can buy.

But there is a lack of contentment. The people are never satisfied. They hunger for purpose in life, and they thirst for peace of mind. Their restless spirits throw them into a kind of perpetual motion, which burns them out but produces nothing. They pursue, they "keep busy," they acquire, but the things of real value have no appeal to them. They and their children seek only the "here and now."

Life is a series of episodes that excite the body but enervate the soul.

God calls through the prophet Isaiah to the people of all times and places:

> Come, all you who are thirsty...
> Come, buy wine and milk
>   without money and without cost.
> Why spend money on what is not bread,
>   and your labor on what does not satisfy?
> Listen, listen to me, and eat what is good,
>   and your soul will delight in the richest of fare.
> Give ear and come to me;
>   hear me, that your soul may live.
>
> *Isa. 55:1-3a*

"Come... listen... hear... that your soul may live" (Isa. 55:1-3).

46
God Heals

"I have seen his ways, but I will heal him;
I will guide him and restore comfort to him,
creating praise on the lips of the mourners in
Israel.
Peace, peace, to those far and near,"
says the Lord. "And I will heal them."

Isa. 57:18-19, *my emphasis*

One of my favorite hymns is:

Come ye disconsolate, where'er ye languish,
Come to the mercy-seat, fervently kneel;
Here bring your wounded hearts, here tell your
 anguish;
Earth has no sorrows that heaven cannot heal.

(Thomas Moore)

Last night I went to sleep singing that song. I had visited a family at a funeral home and overheard the heart-cry of a grief-stricken, guilt-ridden mother. As she mourned the tragic death of a son, she said in her anguish, "I will never get over this." I don't know all that lies beneath that cry, but I do know that "earth has no sorrows that heaven cannot heal."

The above text is set in a context where the loving covenant God is telling His people once again, "I live in a high and holy place, but also with him who is contrite and lowly in spirit, to revive the spirit of the lowly and to revive the heart of the contrite" (v. 15b). God says to us, His people, in all our distresses—whether the trouble is of our own making or not—"Come to Me. Tell Me your anguish. Confess your need of Me—your need to be cleansed and to be renewed. Hold nothing back. And I will heal you, guide you, restore and comfort you, and create praise on your lips." Read again verse 18 above. What beautiful words!

But the Lord wants to make very sure that His children know, *really* know, that there are no incurable wounds, that He is willing and able to heal the deepest hurt. So He keeps on saying to those who come to Him for healing, "Peace, peace... I will heal..." (v. 19).

> Come to the Savior, all,
> Whate'er your burdens be;
> Hear now His loving call,
> "Cast all your care on Me."
> Come, and for every grief
> In Jesus you will find
> A sure and safe relief,
> A loving friend and kind.
>
> *(John M. Wigner)*

47
Well-Watered Gardens

If you do away with the yoke of oppression,
  with the pointing finger and malicious talk,
and if you spend yourselves on behalf of the hungry
  and satisfy the needs of the oppressed,
then your light will rise in the darkness,
  and your night will become like the noonday.
The Lord will guide you always;
  he will satisfy your needs in a sun-scorched land
  and will strengthen your frame.
You will be like a well-watered garden,
  like a spring whose waters never fail.

Isa. 58:9b-11

Who would not like to be "like a well-watered garden"—attractive, colorful, lush, fruitful? Or, "like a spring whose waters never fail"—pure, bubbling, refreshing, constant? Who would not like to be steadily guided, to be completely satisfied, and to feel strength surging through his/her body and spirit every day anew? Fruitful, springing, content, and strong—what a picture of an abundantly happy life!

Such a life is available to God's people. Two conditions are clear from the above passage:

1. "Do away with the yoke of oppression, with the pointing finger and malicious talk" (v. 9b).

But, Lord, You know that we really can't change much in our society. The people who are moving into our neighborhoods are just not "our kind." They cause our whole neighborhood to deteriorate. Many of them are lazy and immoral.

And God asks, "Just what have you done to help them?"

2. "... spend yourselves on behalf of the hungry and satisfy the needs of the oppressed" (v. 10a).

I tithe regularly, Lord; what more do You expect of me? I can't be responsible for all the irresponsibility of others.

And God says, "Spend your *self*—not just your money. I gave you a mind, a heart, and a creative spirit. Use them—thoughtfully, compassionately, and imaginatively to find ways to "satisfy the needs of the oppressed."

Then, and then only, "you will be like a well-watered garden, like a spring whose waters never fail."

How is your garden growing lately?

48
There Was No One to Pray

The Lord looked... He saw...
and He was appalled that there was no one to intercede.

Isa. 59:15b-16a

Conditions among God's people were terrible in Isaiah's day:

> So justice is driven back,
>   and righteousness stands at a distance;
> truth has stumbled in the streets,
>   honesty cannot enter.
> Truth is nowhere to be found,
>   and whoever shuns evil becomes a prey.
>
> Isa. 59:14-15a

The poor were oppressed; the leaders were corrupt; the people were lawless. Anyone who tried to do right was laughed at and persecuted ("preyed upon," v. 15a). Things were going so bad that God was looking around for someone to pray about the mess. He tried to find just one person who was concerned enough to call upon Him to help. But "there was no one to intercede." What a deplorable state! There was not one person who was praying and steadily pleading with God to open the eyes of His people so that they would see their sin, change their ways, and turn from impending disaster and death to a meaningful, beautiful life.

"There was no one to intercede." How far are we from that situation today? The description of Isaiah's time (vv. 14-15) sounds like a page from today's newspaper. And, as we become more aware as to what is going on even in "Christian" circles today, we see the all-pervading, pernicious power of sin. Love has died in many a family; infidelity is rampant; alcohol and drugs have gripped the lives of many; the pursuit of possessions and pleasure has become the driving force in many lives; indifference to God and coldness of spirit characterizes much of our nation and many of our churches.

What must we do? Pray. Intercede. The sin of the lack of intercession is as great as all other sins, for it shows a lack of love. "Far be it from me that I should sin against the Lord by failing to pray for you" (I Sam. 12:23). No, rather, may we heed Isaiah's call: "You who call on the Lord, give yourselves no rest, and give him no rest till he establishes Jerusalem and makes her the praise of the earth" (Isa. 62:6b-7).

Pray that the Lord may bring many in and keep them in.

49
The Justice of Love

For I, the Lord, love justice;
I hate robbery and iniquity.

Isa. 61:8a

Man was created to love God and his neighbor. Such love toward God involves a joyful willingness to do what pleases Him—to obey Him because we love Him and the way of life He has set up. If we love God as a way of life to be embraced, we will want to love our neighbor in a way that shows our love of God. The kind of love God has given us as a model and a prescription is *agape*. Such love is Christ-like—sacrificial and selfless. In everyday relationships it shows itself in the following way. We, by the grace of God, learn to recognize certain God-given resources and potential (gifts) in others. Then, by that same grace, we are willing to "put our lives on the line" to help others develop most fully their God-given resources and thus become the completely beautiful people the Creator intended them to be. When we exercise that kind of love for others, we are practicing justice. When we fail, we are guilty of injustice.

Man has become corrupt at the root of his being. His love is basically self-love. As such, the highest good in life is to serve and to extol himself. There are many areas in which this corruption of the creational moral order becomes apparent. Like a cancer, it begins small but steadily spreads and pervades the whole.

The prophets spoke with penetrating insight into the insidious, subtle workings of injustice and showed how even God's people can be guilty of grave injustices and commit sins which ought to be exposed for what they really are—"robbery" (see above text). The area of injustice the prophets most often warn about is in the use of power. The God-directed way to use power is to lead others, not to lord it over them. The first, God blesses—"I love justice"; the latter, God curses—"I hate robbery."

The Lord puts His people in various situations and invests them with power. Money is power; knowledge is power; all responsibility is power. The rich have power; teachers have power; parents have power; administrators and leaders have power. Power can be used in man's corrupt way—to assert himself and control others for his own ends. Such control is *robbing* another of his or her God-given rights. That way leads to judgment. "I hate robbery." Or, power can be used in God's ordained way—to give oneself so that others may become beautiful people for God's sake. Such use of power is practicing justice, and that way leads to blessing. "I, the Lord, love justice."

50
God's Art with Clay Pots

Yet, O Lord, you are our Father.
We are the clay, you are the potter;
we are all the work of your hand.

Isa. 64:8

God is at work for us and in us. Because He is, we can have confidence and zest for life. The Bible uses different figures of speech to help us understand God's work. In the above passage we see His hands. He is carefully making clay pots for whatever purpose He has in mind. He makes "some pottery for noble purposes and some for common use" (cf. Rom. 9:21). The Potter Himself determines (and He has every right to do so—cf. Isa. 29:16 and Isa. 45:9) what function each one of His products shall have.

But God makes no useless pots. All of God's vessels, whether they are ornamentally wrought or more commonly designed, have God's work to do in God's world. The Potter is always at work. He may remold or reshape some of His pots, and the process may seem almost destructive at times, but God never throws any of His handiwork away.

Why is He such a concerned craftsman who handles us with such care? He is our Father (v. 8a), and as our Father He loves us. As our loving Father, He comes to us in Christ and restores us to our original position of being "little less than God" (Ps. 8:5a, RSV). As our Father, He keeps us from breaking, as fragile clay pots often do. And, as our Father, He invests in us clay pots a treasure—"the light of the knowledge of the glory of God in the face of Christ" (II Cor. 4:6). That is, we as God's clay pots are not only the work of His hands but also in Christ we *become* His very hands and voice in the world today. What a wonder! What grace!

O Lord, thank you that "you are our Father"; that "we are the clay," that "you are the potter." Thank you that "we are all the work of your hand." We know how weak we are, but we know how strong you are. Thank you for making us just as you did, for loving us and sending Christ to remake us, and for giving us work to do—your work in a broken world.

51
Cattle Graze in the Valley of Achor

Sharon will become a pasture for flocks,
 and the Valley of Achor a resting place for
  herds,
for my people who seek me.

Isa. 65:10

Do you remember the Valley of Achor? It had horrible memories for the people of Israel, for it was there that Achan and all his family were stoned for Achan's sin of disobedience—taking spoil from Jericho when God had so firmly commanded that the victors were to take nothing for themselves. Yes, Achan had sinned, and God had to deal with that sin among the company of Israel in a very forceful way so that the people could see the need for unquestioning obedience. Israel had to learn that Canaan would be taken in God's way, and only in that way. Then, once the sin of Achan was purged, God again blessed His people with victory and the comfort of His presence. But the Valley of Achor, the name that means *trouble*, remained desolate.

Another "valley of trouble" in Israel's history was the captivity (see Hos. 2:11ff.). Once again in His justice God must punish His people for their unfaithfulness to Him, for "playing the harlot" with other nations and their gods. But then once more in His mercy God woos His people back. The Babylonian captivity must drive the proud, rebellious people to repentance. Then God stands ready to forgive them and to restore them to fruitfulness.

Look at the idyllic picture of peace and security in our text. From the plain of Sharon in the west to the Valley of Achor in the east, there is an abundance of pasture, of flocks and herds, and rest. Once again the valley of weeping has become a place of springs (cf. Ps. 84:6), and the Valley of Achor (*trouble*) has been changed into a door of hope (cf. Hos. 2:15).

For whom is such a change to take place? For whom do troubles turn to joy and renewed fruitfulness? God says through Isaiah—"for my people who seek me" (v. 10b).

Today the Valley of Achor, the place of trouble, is part of our geography, too. We all know the valleys of affliction when God seems so far away. But if in those valleys we seek the Lord and look to Him for deliverance, there will be pardon, peace, provision, and growth.

Thank the Lord for the place of trouble. Bunyan called it "the most fruitful valley that ever crow flew over." And remember, the Lord's Deliverer, Jesus Christ, is our door of hope in whatever valley we find ourselves. "Call on him while he is near" (Isa. 55:6b).

52
Invitation to Celebration

Shout for joy, O heavens:
  rejoice, O earth;
  burst into song, O mountains!
For the Lord comforts his people
  and will have have compassion on his afflicted ones.

Isa. 49:13

God's work of redemption is so vast that the whole of God's creation is called upon to make His greatness known. The mercy bestowed on mankind is so great that it calls for more praise than human beings are capable of offering.

What special works are noted in chapter 49? The Servant of the Lord will come to deliver God's people and to deal with their enemies. We recognize this Servant as the promised Messiah. The Servant is commissioned to bring back not only the people of Israel, but God states: "I will also make you a light for the Gentiles, that you may bring my salvation to the ends of the earth" (49:6b).

There will be not only an increase in the scope of the Messiah's work but also a change in attitude toward Him. The once "despised and abhorred" One (v. 7) will become One for whom "kings will . . . arise" and "princes will . . . bow down" (v. 7b). From abhorrence to adoration? How did the change come about? "Because of the Lord, who is faithful, the Holy One of Israel, who has chosen you" (v. 7c). Thus, it is not Israel's resilience that changes their state but God's faithfulness that works the wonder. Again, it is God, not man, who changes the hearts of men and the course of history.

And this God knows no obstacles to His power or limits to His love. His Servant, the Messiah, will demonstrate matchless power and boundless love. He will break prison walls (cf. v. 9) and tend the released captives as a shepherd tends a flock of sheep, providing abundant food, spring water, cool shade, and sweet rest (v. 9b-10). Then, this great Shepherd will call. And, look! His sheep will come running from miles away and from all directions—from the north, from the west, and from the extreme south (cf. v. 12).

So, "shout for joy, O heavens; rejoice, O earth; burst into song, O mountains!" (v. 13a) for the Lord redeems, and His redemption knows no bounds!

53
Enjoy God!

*I delight greatly in the Lord;
my soul rejoices in my God.*

Isa. 61:10a

I am often impressed by the emphasis placed on "knowing God" and on "glorifying God," but I am sometimes troubled by the little attention given to "enjoying God." Some of you will remember the first question and answer in the Shorter Catechism of the Westminster Confession. It reads: "What is the chief end of man?" And the answer is: "To glorify God and *to enjoy Him* forever" (my emphasis).

Enjoy God! The Book of Isaiah, though it is a book of judgment, is filled with expressions of joy. It abounds in song and invitations to joy. What is the secret of the prophet? He has found the source of joy and the way to peace. When one lives in the company of God and thinks about the wonders of His ways, the marvels of His grace, the intimacy of His love and care, and then anticipates the prospect of living forever in perfect harmony with God and all His people in a fully restored world, there is joy—irrepressible, boundless joy—joy in the Lord. One such passage from Isaiah pictures such a life of restoration and joy:

> Instead of their shame
>   my people will receive a double portion,
> and instead of disgrace
>   they will rejoice in their inheritance;
> and so they will inherit a double portion in their
>   land,
>   and *everlasting joy will be theirs.*
>
> Isa. 61:7, my emphasis

Note the personal pronoun in the text for this meditation. "*I* delight greatly.... *My* soul rejoices...." Joy is a deeply personal experience. It cannot be borrowed or affected. It is a gift of God, a fruit of the Spirit, and comes to expression from one's most inward being.

> *I* will praise you, O Lord....
> Surely God is *my* salvation;
> *I* will trust and not be afraid.
>
> Isa. 12:1, 2, my emphasis

> O Lord, you are *my* God;
> *I* will exalt you and praise your name....
>
> *Isa. 25:1, my emphasis*

Yes, joy begins when a person recognizes a personal God in his or her personal life.

But there is more. There is not only the subject—the doer who expresses joy—who ought to be considered. There is above all the object—the One who is to receive the expressions of joy and exultation.

> I delight greatly in *the Lord*;
> my soul rejoices in *my* God.
>
> *Isa. 61:10a, my emphasis*

It seems as if I hear an echo to that song. I hear a young woman of faith singing, the woman whom God chose to bring forth the One who would restore harmony to us and bring joy to the world. Listen to Mary sing, and enjoy God with her:

> My soul doth magnify the Lord,
> And my spirit hath rejoiced in God....
>
> *Luke 1:46-47*, KJV

54
New Clothes

I delight greatly in the Lord;
my soul rejoices in my God.
For he has clothed me with garments of salvation
and arrayed me in a robe of righteousness. . . .

Isa. 61:10a

So much of the Bible is about man's need to cover his shame, exposed because of sin. Adam and Eve made fig-leaf aprons for themselves to cover their nakedness. God did not approve of their efforts, but He Himself made clothing for them from skins of animals.

Like Adam and Eve, man has tried throughout the ages to clothe himself, to hide his wrongdoing and cover his inadequacies. He has developed systems of thought by which he attempts to explain away sin. He has tried to convince himself and others that he can produce lasting good and thus make himself look better.

But down deep man knows better. He knows that he cannot clothe himself—that he cannot save himself by anything he produces himself. This truth God has brought to man over and over, and when he accepts it, he sees that his only hope is in God and in what He provides. God comes to us by sending Jesus into the world to take away our sin and shame, and He then, as it were, gives us new clothes—the righteousness of Christ. So now redeemed people stand before God in "garments of salvation" and "robes of righteousness."

These new clothes are pictured in our text. The deliverance from captivity is a symbol of man's redemption from sin—God's work of salvation. The garments of which the prophet speaks are the new clothes God gives His people to wear as they go out into the world to tell the good news that God did for man what man could never do for himself—clothe himself—save himself. And these new clothes will be the white robes (cf. Rev. 19:8) we wear in heaven—as the bride of our loving, eternal Bridegroom.

> By the sea of crystal saints in glory stand,
> Myriads in number, drawn from every land.
> Robed in white apparel, washed in Jesus' blood,
> They now reign in heaven with the Lamb of God.
> *(William Kuipers, 1933)*

55
A Worship Service with Themes from Isaiah

The material found on the following pages may be used as separate devotional pieces but may also be used as a unit and thus constitute a complete worship service. The reader will note the divisions of the liturgy: salutation, hymn of praise and prayer, call to worship; repentance, reawakening, redirection, reassurance and renewal, and rededication.

> Arise, shine. For your light has come,
> and the glory of the Lord rises upon you.
> *Isa. 60:1*

> Awake, my soul, and with the sun
> Thy daily stage of duty run;
> Shake off dull sloth, and joyful rise
> To pay thy morning sacrifice.
>
> Lord, I my vows to Thee renew,
> Disperse my sins as morning dew;
> Guard my first springs of tho't and will,
> And with Thyself my spirit fill.
>
> Direct, control, suggest, this day,
> All I design, or do, or say;
> That all my pow'rs with all their might,
> In Thy sole glory may unite.
>
> *(Tune: Tallis Canon)*

CALL TO WORSHIP

Come, let us go up to the mountain of the Lord,
 to the house of the God of Jacob.

HE WILL TEACH US HIS WAYS,
 SO THAT WE MAY WALK IN HIS PATHS.

The law will go out from Zion,
 the word of the Lord from Jerusalem.

COME, O HOUSE OF JACOB,
 LET US WALK IN THE LIGHT OF THE
  LORD.

Isa. 2:3, 5

In repentance and rest is your salvation. . . .
The Lord longs to be gracious to you;
 he rises to show you compassion.
For the Lord is a God of justice.
 Blessed are all who wait for him.

Isa. 30:15a, 18

O LORD, BE GRACIOUS TO US;
 WE LONG FOR YOU.
BE OUR STRENGTH EVERY MORNING,
 OUR SALVATION IN TIME OF DISTRESS.

Isa. 33:2

He will be the sure foundation for your times,
 a rich store of salvation and wisdom and
  knowledge;
 the fear of the Lord is the key to this treasure.

Isa. 33:6

REPENTANCE

Seek the Lord while he may be found;
 call on him while he is near.

Let the wicked forsake his way
 and the evil man his thoughts.
Let him turn to the Lord, and he will have mercy
 on him,
 and to our God, for he will freely pardon.

Isa. 55:6-7

O GOD, WE TURN TO YOU ANEW, JUST AS YOU HAVE COMMANDED US TO DO.

Hear our confessions, Father.

We often tame the gospel and leash its power.
 Because we flinch from the demands of Christ,
 we make for ourselves a religion of caution and comfort.
 We fear pain and shun our cross.
 We prefer to sit because
  it takes effort and courage to stand.

O LORD, HAVE MERCY ON US.

We corrupt our profession with inconsistencies
and subtly decieve ourselves.

We sing, "My God, how great Thou art,"
but go on putting self and its pleasures
in the center of our world.

We recite our creeds; we say that the body of Christ
 is one
and that no member is greater than another.
Yet we consciously wound fellow Christians
with cutting words and unforgiving stares.
We sometimes separate limbs from Christ's body
with our superiority and prejudice.

We keep telling ourselves that we can be a salting
 salt
even though we flee from society
and live in closed communities.

DELIVER US FROM OURSELVES. HELP US TO BE HONEST.

We let prosperity and the pace of life dull our senses.

> Today millions hunger; children starve.
> We have so much, but we give so little.
>
> The sick moan; the lonely and the troubled cry.
> We are too busy to hear.

LORD, MAKE US AWARE. TEACH US TO CARE.

We have lost our balance of intake and output.

> We suffer spiritual indigestion.
> We are fed so much and we exercise so little.
> We are so stuffed with the words of Christianity that we have little spirit for the works.

O GOD, REFRESH US BY THY GRACE.

We lack spiritual outlook and adventure.

> We live in an exciting age of revolution.
> New nations are being born.
> People long down-trodden are rising to claim their heritage as bearers of the divine image.
> Populations are expanding.
> Societies and cultures are maturing.
> The awesome world of space is opening before us.
> But we are not excited.
> We stand back and let non-Christian forces shape the world.
> We fear the untried. Change threatens us.
> We withdraw from new ideas.
> We cry, "Give us only answers. Questions disturb us."
> We exclaim with the poet: "The world is charged with the grandeur of God."

But we are afraid to explore that grandeur—
To stretch out our hands and touch that
  charge—
Lest it shock us and shake our little systems.

AWAKEN US, LORD. REVIVE AND
QUICKEN ALL OUR POWERS.

REAWAKENING

As in the days of Isaiah, God's commands arouse us.

"Arise, cry out in the night . . . lift your hands to
  God."
"Arise and go, for this is no place to rest."

"Awake, Awake, O Zion, clothe yourself with
  strength."

Isa. 52:1

WE WILL ARISE AND GO—**IN YOUR
STRENGTH**, O GOD.

Wake, awake, for night is flying,
The watchmen on the heights are crying,
  Awake, Jerusalem, arise!
Midnight's solemn hour is tolling,
His chariot wheels are nearer rolling;
He comes; prepare, ye virgins wise;
Rise up with willing feet;
Go forth, the Bridegroom meet;
  Alleluia!
Bear through the night your well-trimmed light,
Speed forth to join the marriage rite.

Zion hears the watchmen singing,
And all her heart with joy is springing;
  She wakes, she rises from her gloom.

Forth her Bridegroom comes, all glorious,
The strong in grace, in truth victorious;
Her star is risen, her light is come.
All hail, Thou precious One,
Lord Jesus, God's dear Son!
   Alleluia!
The joyful call we answer all,
And follow to the nuptial hall.

Lamb of God, the heavens adore Thee,
And men and angels sing before Thee
   With harp and cymbal's clearest tone.
By the pearly gates in wonder
We stand, and swell the voice of thunder
In bursts of choral melody.
To mortal eyes and ears
What glory now appears!
   Alleluia!
We raise the song, we swell the throng,
To praise Thee ages all along.

(Philipp Nicolai, 1599)

REDIRECTION

I am the Lord your God,
   who teaches you what is best for you,
   who directs you in the way you should go.

Isa. 48:17b

God's Word redirects us.

For each of the wrong ways we confess,
God marks out a right way.

We confess that we cling to self and shun our cross.

"Jesus then said to his disciples, 'If anyone wishes to be a follower of mine, he must leave self behind; he must take up his cross and come with me. Whoever cares for his own safety is lost; but if a man will let himself be lost for my sake, he will find his true self.'"

MAY WE BE DOERS OF THE WORD AND NOT HEARERS ONLY.

We confess that we are often not a unifying power in the church and a saving salt in the world.

"Dear brothers, if a Christian is overcome by some sin, you who are godly should gently and humbly help him back onto the right path, remembering that next time it might be one of you who is in the wrong."

"Have salt in yourselves and be at peace with one another."

MAY WE BE DOERS OF THE WORD AND NOT HEARERS ONLY.

We say we know not how to care and to share.

"Then shall the King say to them on his right hand, 'You have my Father's blessing. Come, possess the kingdom... For when I was hungry, you gave me food. When I was sick, you came to my help...
I tell you this: anything you did for one of my brothers here, however humble, you did for me.'"

MAY WE BE DOERS OF THE WORD AND NOT HEARERS ONLY.

We admit that we dare too little for God.

Then God replies,
"Be fruitful... fill the earth and subdue it."
"Buy up opportunities for service."
"Live as free men..."

HELP US, LORD, TO RECLAIM THE WORLD.

REASSURANCE AND RENEWAL

I, the Lord, have called you in righteousness;
    I will take hold of your hand.
I will keep you and will make you
    to be a covenant for the people
    and a light for the Gentiles....

Isa. 42:6

God's promises assure us.

IF YOU THEN, THOUGH YOU ARE EVIL, KNOW HOW TO GIVE GOOD GIFTS TO YOUR CHILDREN, HOW MUCH MORE WILL YOUR FATHER IN HEAVEN GIVE THE HOLY SPIRIT TO THOSE WHO ASK HIM!

The Spirit equips us.

HE ENLIGHTENS AND ENLIVENS US.
HE UPROOTS SELF AND FEAR AND
    IMPLANTS CHRIST AND FAITH.
IN HIS LIGHT WE SEE AND HOPE.
IN HIS POWER WE LIVE AND DARE.

Come, then, stiffen your drooping arms and shaking knees, and keep your steps from wavering.
Heb. 12:12, NEB; *cf. Isa. 35:3*

THE KINGDOM WE ARE GIVEN IS UNSHAKABLE... WE ARE RECEIVING A KINGDOM THAT CANNOT BE SHAKEN....
Heb. 12:28

REDEDICATION

God of the prophets! Bless us, prophets' sons;
Elijah's mantle o'er Elisha cast;
Each age its solemn task may claim but once;
Make each one nobler, stronger than the last.

Anoint us prophets! Make our ears attent
To Thy divinest speech, our hearts awake
To human need; our lips make eloquent
To gird the right and every evil break.

Anoint us priests! Strong intercessors, Lord!
Anoint us with the Spirit of Thy Son;
Ours not a jeweled crown, a blood-stained sword;
Ours, by sweet love, for Christ a kingdom won.

Make us apostles! Heralds of Thy cross.
Forth may we go to tell all realms Thy grace,
Inspired of Thee, may we count all but loss,
And stand at last with joy before Thy face.
(Denis Wortman, 1884, alt.)